The EASTERN SIERRA

CALIFORNIA NEVADA

W9-BEM-389

PYRAMID LAKE

RENO SPARKS
Truckee River

TRUCKEE

VIRGINIA CITY

INCLINE VILLAGE

CARSON CITY

DONNER MEMORIAL STATE PARK

TAHOE CITY

LAKE TAHOE

MINDEN

EMERALD BAY STATE PARK

SOUTH LAKE TAHOE

50

MARKLEEVILLE

Carson Pass

Monitor Pass

Topaz Lake

Walker River

Ebbetts Pass

Sonora Pass

BRIDGEPORT

Twin Lakes

BODIE STATE HISTORIC PARK

YOSEMITE NATIONAL PARK

Hetch Hetchy Reservoir

167

MONO LAKE

Tioga Pass

LEE VINING

120 Mt. Dana el. 13,053

MONO CRATERS

120

TOULOMNE MEADOWS

JUNE LAKE

YOSEMITE VILLAGE

140

Minaret Summit

203

DEVILS POSTPILE NATIONAL MONUMENT

MAMMOTH LAKES

Mammoth Mtn el. 11,053

CROWLEY LAKE

6

BENTON

Boundary Peak el. 13,940

95

White Mtn el. 14,246

ANCIENT BRISTLECONE FOREST

CHALFANT VALLEY

LAWS

Westgard Pass

BISHOP

168

BIG PINE

Owens River

Wheeler Peak el. 13,063

GREAT BASIN NATIONAL PARK (Eastern Nevada)

BAKER
488

SIERRA NEVADA

KINGS CANYON NATIONAL PARK

INDEPENDENCE

Mt. Williamson el. 14,375

MANZANAR

LONE PINE

Mt. Whitney el. 14,494

SEQUOIA NATIONAL PARK

Owens Valley

EUREKA SAND DUNES

SCOTTYS CASTLE

DEATH VALLEY NATIONAL MONUMENT

FURNACE CREEK

DEATH VALLEY JUNCTION

Telescope Peak el. 11,049

Badwater el. -280

136

Owens Lake (Bed)

190

OLANCHA

395

Kern River

Sca Fork Kern River

LITTLE LAKES

TRONA

N

CALIFORNIA REPUBLIC

RED ROCK CANYON STATE PARK

395

CALIFORNIA

NEVADA

Linda Trujillo

Bands of light break behind Mt. Whitney and the Wheeler Crest.
LARRY PROSOR

Exploring the
Eastern Sierra
California & Nevada

A Companion Press Book

by Mark A. Schlenz

© 1990 Companion Press
Santa Barbara, California

No part of this publication may be reproduced in
any form without permission.

Edited by Jane Freeburg
Designed by Lucy Brown
Pictorial map by Linda Trujillo

Printed and bound in Korea
Through Bolton Associates
San Rafael, California

ISBN 0-944197-12-4

Contents

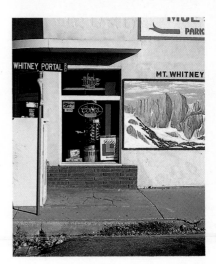

Opposite: Ancient bristlecone in the White Mountains foregrounds distant Sierra skyline.
LARRY ULRICH

From top:

After snowmelt, a fragile snow plant blooms brilliantly on the forest floor.
DENNIS FLAHERTY

A weathered barn stands near Bridgeport.
BOB LEROY

Sheep graze near Mono Lake.
GARY MOON

Downtown Lone Pine. Turn left to behold Mt. Whitney, highest peak in the continental United States.
JEFF NICHOLAS

*Opposite: Late afternoon
light illumines a rocky
crest in the John Muir
Wilderness.*
PAT O'HARA

*Above: Photographing a
high alpine lake in the
Dusy Basin.*
PAT O'HARA

CHAPTER ONE:

The Range of Light: Discover the Eastern Sierra

In 1776 Father Pedro Font, a Franciscan missionary with the Anza expedition, looked east from a hill near the San Francisco Bay toward distant peaks and saw *"una gran sierra nevada,"* a great range of snowy mountains. In 1866, a young John Muir, en route to Yosemite from San Francisco, also viewed the snowy peaks across California's central valley. Even more impressed at first sight with their sunny brilliance than their icy whiteness, it seemed to Muir that "the Sierra should be called not the Nevada, or Snowy Range, but the Range of Light."

During the ninety years that passed between Font's and Muir's introductory glimpses of the looming mountain range, other famous explorer adventurers — and many more unnamed pioneers, miners, and settlers — encountered even more dramatic first impressions of the Sierra Nevada as they sought overland routes west to the Pacific. For the overland California-bound traveler, the magnificent up-lifted escarpment of the Eastern Sierra was an over-whelming wall reaching from the floor of the Great Basin to the clouds. After a continent's-breadth of obstacles, this final mountain barrier loomed as an ultimate challenge before such legendary men as Jedediah Smith, John C. Fremont, and Kit Carson, as well as the less fortunate families of the Donner Party and Death Valley's forty-niners. Their stories — told by historic remnants of their struggles still visible on the landscape and the legends that have grown about them — tell tales of heroic human struggle in an incredible wilderness.

Pioneer legends, however, together with the sagas of the Indian peoples who have lived in this land for centuries, occupy only a brief moment of time in the natural history of these magnificent mountains.

The Eastern Escarpment

Geologists say the tilted fault-block range of the Sierra Nevada formed ten to twenty million years ago when an enormous piece of the earth's crust rose thousands of feet along a series of faults and tilted westward to create a mountain range with broad, gentle western slopes and a steep, precipitous eastern escarpment. More than 400 miles long and between 60 to 80 miles wide, the Sierra covers a region larger than the combined areas of the French, Swiss, and Italian Alps; the Sierra Nevada stretches further than any continuous mountain range in the continental United States. This massive mountain barrier forming the western boundary of the Great Basin and separates the arid lands to the east from the less dry valleys of central and northern California — and the climatic influences of the Pacific Ocean.

In the southern Sierra, along the west side of Owens Valley, the most impressive span of the eastern escarpment extends in an unbroken ridge 70 miles in length. Numerous peaks rise from 9,000 to 10,800 feet above the 3,500 to 4,000 foot elevation of the valley floor. This formidable cresting of the southern Sierra reaches its strongest thrust at 14,496-foot Mt. Whitney, the highest mountain peak in the continental United States. North of Bishop the peaks of the main crest decrease in average elevations and the valleys rise. The unbroken escarpment of the Southern Sierra gives way to a series of spur ranges branching north and east from the main crest and separating the higher valleys along Highway 395. Finally the Carson Range branches north from the Sierra crest and forms the Tahoe Basin, an impressive alpine setting for the turquoise jewel of Lake Tahoe — the "Lake of the Sky."

Great ice caps blanketed the region of the High Sierra south of Lake Tahoe during the Pleistocene Epoch, about three to ten million years ago. Evidence of the once-great glaciers can be seen everywhere in this spectacular landscape of jagged peaks, mirroring lakes, alpine meadows, ice-scoured gorges and high, rocky windswept basins. Elegantly sculpted cliffs that tower over broad valley floors, vast expanses of highly polished rock, and curving ridges of rock debris attest to the tremendous carving power of the moving ice sheets.

About three million years ago volcanic activity began along the east side of the Sierra south of Mono Lake. Eruptions around Mammoth Lakes some 700,000 years ago climaxed with a tremendous explosion from Glass Mountain. The blast's inferno scorched a 350-square-mile area in Long Valley and covered it with 500 feet of volcanic ash. The hexagonal, basaltic columns of Devils Postpile, the blasted volcano of Mammoth Mountain, the Mono Craters, and numerous other volcanic features on the landscape give dramatic testimony to more recent and continued geothermic activity in the Eastern Sierra.

Tremendous mountain-shaping forces of geologic uplifting, glaciation, and volcanic activity have joined powers in the Eastern Sierra Nevada to build and carve a range unparalleled in its picturesque majesty. These mountains occupy some of the largest roadless areas in the 48 states and contain some of the grandest scenery in the West. Above treeline, mazes of lichen-covered rocks border alpine gardens of arctic-adapted plants and flowers watered by melting snows. Below the alpine zones, conifer forests blanket upper slopes of the Eastern Sierra

and follow the stream-courses downward. Further downslope, pinyon-juniper woodland and sagebrush scrub extend into the valleys at the feet of the range. The streams of the Eastern Sierra never flowed to the ocean, but met their destinies in shallow, spreading desert lakes beneath billowing clouds and brilliant skies.

Towering mountains of the Eastern Sierra sweep this landscape with their shadows while sunlight dances in endless play among their lofty peaks. John Muir thought the Sierra Nevada was the most divinely beautiful of any mountain-chain he had ever seen. After he had spent many years "bathing in its glorious floods of light, seeing the sunbursts of morning among the icy peaks, the noonday radiance on the trees and rocks and snow, the flush of alpenglow, and a thousand dashing waterfalls with their marvellous abundance of irised spray," Muir still believed the Sierra Nevada to be, above all other mountains, the Range of Light.

Exploring the Eastern Sierra

Climates and panoramas of the Eastern Sierra Nevada change rapidly with shifts in elevations and seasons. The faces of the mountains take on new expressions with each perspective of the viewer and with every shift in the angle of the sun's lighting. From the arid desert floors of the California and Nevada borderlands to the summits of the Pacific Crest, an amazing diversity of plants and animals has adapted to challenging conditions ranging from days of relentless sun to long months of ice and snow. Human visitors to the area must also adapt to

Intense alpine sun melts "suncups" up to two feet deep. There is no easy way to hike in this terrain!
JEFFREY G. SIPRESS

Top: The Palisade Crest, longest ridge of 14,000-foot peaks in the Sierra, looms over the Owens Valley.
ED COOPER

Inset, top: A yellow-bellied marmot, Marmota flaviventris, *scouts his granite rockfield habitat.*
DENNIS FLAHERTY

Center: Desert sands sparkle at Eureka Sand Dunes.
DENNIS FLAHERTY

Bottom: Intense heat formed this pocket-patterned volcanic rock at Mono Craters.
BOB LEROY

the differing conditions of the terrain and the constantly changing patterns of heat, wind, rain, and snow. Indians inhabiting the region for centuries often moved whole villages higher into the mountains in the summers, leaving the hotter lowlands to seek more plentiful water, wildlife, and plants further upslope.

Extensive travel in the Eastern Sierra has always involved a mixture of adventure with the pleasures of its scenery. Indians of the Mono Lake area sometimes traveled clear across the Sierra during the summers to trade their pinyon nut harvests for acorns with the tribes of the western slopes. Early explorers Captain John C. Fremont and Kit Carson successfully crossed the range near Carson Pass in the winter of 1844, but later settlers, like the ill-fated Donner party in 1847, sometimes met with extreme hardship or perished attempting winter crossings. Even today the Tioga and Sonora Pass roads close for much of the winter. (Check the status of Walker, Monitor, Carson, and Donner Passes passes before travelling.) Highway 395 provides reliable access to much of this year-round vacationland. Its remote reaches may be explored, depending upon the season, via jeep road or snow mobile, on horseback or on skis, by bicycle or — like the earliest visitors in this Range of Light — by foot.

CHAPTER TWO:
The Cresting Sierra

Opposite: Cactus among the Alabama Hills near the foot of Lone Pine Peak.
LARRY ULRICH

Above: An abandoned rail station near Lone Pine.
BOB LEROY

Nestled between the tallest peaks of the Eastern Sierra to the west, and the older Inyo and White Mountains to the east, lies the Owens Valley, named in 1845 by John C. Fremont for one of his expedition captains. White Mountain, to the northeast, reaches well over 14,000 feet and competes with Mt. Whitney in height to make the Owens Valley one of the deepest — and most scenic — valleys in the world. Incredible geologic forces shaped the tremendous proportions of this valley. The last remnants of Owens Lake once belonged to an immense inland sea, as large as the Mediterranean, covering much of the Great Basin and leaving fresh-water fossils and shells on the slopes of the White Mountains up to elevations of 3,000 feet. Long periods of volcanic activity formed Red Hill and other impressive cinder cones along the west side of the valley, and vast lava beds have covered much of the valley floor at various times. Fault scarps and other evidence of major earthquakes, including the historic quake of 1872 that claimed the lives of many valley residents, are plainly visible from the highway. Above the ancient lake beds and the river, above the dark volcanic rock of the Alabama Hills, worn and broken by the forces of erosion, mountains struggle ever sky-ward in sheer granite leaps toward the highest ridges of the cresting Sierra.

Owens Valley

Approaching Owens Valley from the junction of US Highway 395 and State Highway 14, the traveler sees the eastern front of the Sierra Nevada begin its climb higher and higher toward the north. Evidence of prehistoric volcanic activity marks the landscape along the highway . Lava cliffs around the spring-fed waters of Little Lake cooled and fractured into columnar structures similar to those found further north at Devils Postpile National Monument. To the east the scorched and barren slopes of the Coso Range tell of their fiery volcanic past. Between Little Lake and Red Hill a short side road to the east leads to a spectacular hundred-foot, dry waterfall: deep pot holes, stream-polished rock surfaces, and the gorge itself were all cut into the lavas by a glacial Owens River. Nearby Red Hill formed when pebble-sized fragments of highly porous lava were thrown explosively from a volcanic vent and then piled into a massive cinder cone. North of Red Hill the highway enters Rose Valley where a pleasant grove of cottonwood trees shades a roadside rest area at Coso Junction.

Entering the town of Olancha, the shimmering white, alkali flats of Owens Lake become visible stretching across the floor of the Owens Valley. In 1913, the Los Angeles Aqueduct Project diverted Owens River from the lake

which once reached depths of 30 feet and covered 100 square miles. After particularly wet seasons water may still cover parts of the lake floor for a year or more before evaporating. The increasing steepness of the Sierra front reaches a height of 12,123 feet at Olancha Peak, almost eight and a half thousand feet above the once-lake-front towns of Olancha and Cartago.

In the 1870s steamboats operated commercially on Owens Lake. A mile east of the highway below Cottonwood Canyon stand historic kilns which once shipped charcoal across the lake to the eastern-shore town of Keeler and the famous Cerro Gordo Mines. In 1870, Cerro Gordo produced over 17 million dollars of silver-lead bullion. A side-trip loop around the eastern side of Owens Lake leaves Olancha on Route 190 and rejoins Highway 395 south of Lone Pine on Route 136. At the north end of the lake, look for the parallel shoreline marks, like bathtub rings, that indicate historic water levels of the vanishing lake: those near the lake resulted from the diversion of the Owens River in 1913, but higher shoreline features may be 10,000 to 15,000 years old.

Mt. Whitney

North of Owens Lake the Alabama Hills begin to rise west of the highway. Just south of Lone Pine the eastern bedrock face of the Alabama Hills provides an impressive back-drop for Lake Diaz, a large pond formed when a strip of land between two faults dropped during the 1872 earthquake. The metavolcanic rock of the Alabama Hills may look familiar — it provided natural backdrops for numerous Hollywood Western and adventure movies. A scenic drive from Lone Pine to the Whitney Portals, dramatically featured in the 1948 movie classic *High Sierra* starring Humphrey Bogart, winds through the weirdly sculpted rock formations of the Alabama Hills to approach the base of the the cresting Sierra's supreme pin-nacle, Mt. Whitney. A well-traveled trail now leads from the Portals to the rocky peak first climbed by mountaineers in 1873.

Less adventurous travelers may view the lofty 14,496-foot summit of Mt. Whitney quite well from the 18-hole Mt. Whitney Golf Course

An aerial view of Owens Lake.
BILL DEWEY

in Lone Pine or from the Eastern Sierra Interpretive Association's Interagency Visitor Center. Located at the junction of Highway 395 and the Route 136 turnoff to Death Valley, the Interagency Visitor Center provides a complete source of information about the Eastern Sierra and surrounding country, from books detailing the region's natural and human histories to up-to-date reports on vital weather, road, and campground conditions.

West of the highway, just north of Lone Pine, a monument commemorates the victims of the devastating earthquake of 1872. On March 26, a temblor that may have been stronger even than the San Francisco quake of 1906 shook the Owens Valley and nearly destroyed the small town of Lone Pine. Twenty-seven persons died and land fell from four to twelve feet along a fault paralleling the highway at the feet of the Alabama Hills. On the exposed and windswept rise of an older scarp, the monument lists the names of a few of the sixteen people buried in a common grave, now surrounded by a wooden picket fence. The names of the rest of the victims — from French, Irish, Chilean, Mexican, and Native American ancestries — may never be known. From the lonely grave site, look a quarter-mile to the south and the west to see the scarp of the 1872 quake plainly visible behind the town. Watch for the numerous folds and wrinkles of earthquake scarps from various ages as you travel along the valley north of Lone Pine.

Between the towns of Lone Pine and Independence another monument commemorates the victims of a very different type of human tragedy. Before completion of the Owens River diversions, Manzanar was once a fertile fruit

Above: Lone Pine Peak wears a shawl of clouds. Indian legend named the peak Oppapago, "The Weeper." Jagged Wheeler Crest peeks beneath the clouds at right.
CHUCK PLACE

Center: Pioneer relics of the Owens Valley are preserved at the Eastern California Museum in Independence.
CARA MOORE

Bottom: Contemporary cowboys at work against a backdrop of Mt. Whitney.
CARA MOORE

producing center. ("*Manzanar*" is Spanish for apple.) Its rich orchards produced some of the finest apples ever grown in California. During World War II 10,000 Japanese-Americans citizens were separated from their homes and confined in an internment camp occupying this site. Today the gatehouse, a few cement foundations, and some struggling trees remind visitors of a humiliating phase of our nation's history. Directly east, behind the camp, Mt. Williamson looms over the abandoned orchards and ruins.

The hulking massif of 14,375-foot Mt. Williamson dominates much of the Eastern Sierra skyline north of Lone Pine. Southbound travelers on Highway 395 enjoy superb views of this giant from as far away as the Poverty Hills above Independence.

The Inyo Mountains forming the eastern rim of this portion of the Owens Valley thronged with mining activity around the turn of the century. Travel east three miles on Mazourka Canyon road at the south edge of the town of Independence to see the picturesque remains of the Kearsarge mining operation perched on a prominent scarp in the alluvium at the feet of the Inyos. On the low skyline of the Inyos to the north of Kearsarge, the eighty foot tall granite column of Paiute Monument points to the heavens. Known to the Indians as *Winnedumah*, this ancient landmark has been the source of many local legends. Sharp eyes may spot the singular monolith on the ridgeline from the highway north of Independence.

Independence

Taking its new name from nearby Camp Independence — established on Independence Day, July 4, 1862 — the small town of Independence, once called Little Pine, has been the seat of Inyo County since February 3, 1866. The Old Western past of Independence survives today in the architecture of the town's historic buildings and in the comprehensive collections of Owens Valley memorabilia housed at the Eastern California Museum on Grant Street. Museum exhibits display Shoshone and Paiute basketry, beadwork, and arrowheads as well as unusual mementos from the World War II relocation camp for Japanese-Americans at Manzanar. Behind the museum a recreated "Little Pine Village" features weathered buildings and antique farming, mining, and shop equipment from all over the county against a scenic backdrop of the Sierra. Train buffs will want to inspect the museum's narrow gauge "Slim Princess" Locomotive #18 located at Dehy Park.

Originally built at Camp Independence in 1872, the "Commander's House" now sits on Highway 395 at the corner of Edwards and Main

Top: Sculpted rock frames Inyo County's Courthouse, in Independence.
BOB LEROY

Left: Mt. Williamson rises behind the monument at Manzanar, a silent memorial to the 10,000 Japanese Americans interned here during World War II.
KEN BIRCHIM

14

Top: Mt. Whitney Fish Hatchery, built of local stone.
KEN BIRCHIM

Inset: Hatchery trout.
JEFF NICHOLAS

streets. The former home of Mary Austin, celebrated author of *Land of Little Rain*, still stands in Independence, as does the oldest home in Inyo County — the Edwards House built by Thomas Edwards in 1865. An extraordinary example of uniquely Eastern Sierra architecture, the Mt. Whitney Fish Hatchery — built in 1916 from local uncut granite boulders and guaranteed "not to crumble until the mountains shall fall" — is just north of town.

Between Independence and Big Pine dramatic traces of the various geologic forces of mountain formation are plainly visible. Several cinder cones give further evidence of large-scale volcanic activity while a discernable scarp of the 1872 earthquake parallels the west side of the highway running north from the Poverty Hills and along the base of Crater Mountain. Above Big Pine, the cresting Sierra gathers itself up into its longest ridge of connected 14,000-foot peaks — known as the Palisade Crest. The Palisade Glacier, largest glacier in the Sierra, lies at the base of the impressive wall of the Palisades. A steep road up Big Pine Canyon, west of town, climbs switchbacks across massive glacial moraines of the ice-age as it winds its way to Glacier Lodge, campgrounds, and trailheads leading to the Palisade Glacier itself.

Traveling east out of Big Pine, visitors may follow Westgard Pass (Highway 162) into the White Mountains and the Ancient Bristlecone Pine Forest. The partly unpaved road from Westgard Pass to the remote Patriarch Grove offers unequaled views of the cresting Sierra from high across the Owens Valley. Specimens of bristlecone pine (*Pinus longavea*) found in the Patriarch Grove are among the oldest living organisms on earth. Adapted to harsh exposure to sun, wind, ice, and desert dryness as well as to the alkali soil of dolemitic limestone found in the high and isolated White Mountains, these fantastically twisted and sculpted trees inhabit one of the most hostile and mysterious landscapes in the West.

Bishop

Nestled between the White Mountains and the towering Sierras as the northern end of the Owens Valley, the town of Bishop provides ample accommodations and a base for numerous outdoor activities including hiking, skiing, fishing, bicycling, mountain climbing, camping, photography, canoeing and hang gliding. Day adventures in the Bishop area may range from a visit to the rock art petroglyphs in nearby Chalfant Valley, to a drive into the Ancient Bristlecone Pine Forest, to an afternoon picnic and walk around a high Sierra lake in Bishop Creek Canyon. Once a year, on Memorial Day

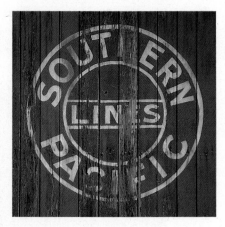

weekend, this quiet desert community throngs with packers, tourists, and beasts as Bishop, California becomes the "Mule Capital of the World" during its annual Mule Days Celebration. Started in 1969 by Eastern High Sierra packers who wanted to get together for a good time and initiate their summer packing season, Bishop's Mule Days has grown to enormous popularity and features as many as 600 mules competing in more than 94 events.

Two interesting museums preserve diverse aspects of Bishop's historic past. The Paiute Shoshone Indian Cultural Center on West Line Street is dedicated by the Indian people of the Owens Valley to sharing the heritage, traditions, and art of their ancestors — "observant, resourceful, and practical" peoples who lived for ages in harmony with this land — with local residents and visitors. Five miles from downtown Bishop north on Highway 6, the Laws Railroad Museum and Historical Site preserves the last narrow gauge railroad depot to operate west of the Rocky Mountains. The Depot Building, originally built in 1883, and surrounding structures now house impressive collections of narrow gauge equipment. "Slim Princess" Locomotive #98 rests in the railyard on its original tracks, and young visitors are still welcome to ring its bell.

From Bishop, the Pacific Crest of the Sierra turns and runs more sharply to the north, forming Round and Pleasant Valleys. Heading up Highway 395's Sherwin Grade from these gentle pasture lands, travelers enjoy inviting glimpses beyond a sweeping alluvial floodplain and Bishop Creek Canyon into the very heart of the Sierra. In afternoon brightness or in the slanting light of evening or dawn, brilliantly etched against a field of cobalt blue or veiled by mists and clouds of a clearing storm, few sights rival the grandeur of these most majestic of mountains.

Top, left: Narrow gauge rail lines once carried rich ore and supplies through the Eastern Sierra region. Rail history is preserved at the Laws Railroad Museum near Bishop.
JEFF BROUWS

Top, right: Weathered logo on a freight car.
CARA MOORE

Center: The Slim Princess, a narrow gauge locomotive, on display at the Laws Railroad Museum.
DENNIS FLAHERTY

Bottom: Petroglyphs found in Chalfant Valley, rock art of ancient peoples of the Eastern Sierra.
DENNIS FLAHERTY

Ancient Bristlecone Pine Forest

Travel over Westgard Pass east of Big Pine to visit this high windswept landscape, home of 4,000-year-old trees. Viewpoints command vistas of the Sierra Nevada Range to the west.

Top: The Patriarch Grove at sunrise.
LARRY ULRICH

Far Right: Sculpted by wind and weather, the hardy bristlecone pines are among the world's oldest living things. This venerable tree frames a view of the Owens Valley and Sierra Nevada Range.
BOB LEROY

Inset: Sharp bristles on the cone distinguish the bristlecone pine.
BOB LEROY

Death Valley National Monument

Above: The view from Zabriskie Point encompasses eroded badlands of Golden Canyon, the salt-encrusted floor of Death Valley, and snow-capped Telescope Peak.
LARRY ULRICH

Far Left: An expanse of dried, cracked mud at the Race Track.
FRED HIRSCHMANN

Inset: Early morning light on sand dunes at Mesquite Flats.
JEFF NICHOLAS

For all the toll the desert takes of a man it gives compensations, deep breaths, deep sleep, and the communion of the stars.

—MARY AUSTIN
THE LAND OF LITTLE RAIN
1903

Top: Scottys Castle, built in the 1920s, was once a summer home for Albert Johnson of Chicago and his colorful friend, Death Valley Scotty.
LARRY PROSOR

Center: Minerals stain colorful sculpted hills at Artists Palette.
CARA MOORE

Lower Right: Salt-pan and the tortured surface of Devils Speedway.
DEANNA DULEN

CHAPTER THREE

Heart of the Sierra

Opposite: Early fall colors along McGee Creek.
FRANK S. BALTHIS

Above: Canoeing across Convict Lake.
LARRY PROSOR

Climbing up from Round Valley to Tom's Place, Highway 395 ascends through pinyon pine and juniper woodlands to enter Mono County and the heartland of the Eastern Sierra. Road cuts expose the peculiar rosy rock strata known to geologists as the Bishop tuff, evidence of volcanic activity in this region. Startling views of Mt. Ritter and Mt. Banner — and the serrated ridge of the Minarets in the northern distance — greet travelers at the summit of the Sherwin Grade. Nearby Tom's Place, a roadhouse with considerable local color near the entrance to the Rock Creek and Little Lakes Valley areas, provides refreshment.

North, a few miles further, the blue sheet of Lake Crowley spread across the grassy bed of Long Valley. The Glass Mountains fold gently along the skyline to the east. Hilton and McGee Creeks, the mouths of their canyons filled with huge glacial moraines, empty into the valley from the Sierra high country. Further north, en route toward Mammoth Lakes on Highway 395, a side road to the west heads up to Convict Lake where, in 1871, lawmen shot it out with escapees from a Carson City prison. Another side road to the east crosses the valley to an active geothermal site at Hot Creek. Near the Casa Diablo Hot Springs, where winter visitors occasionally glimpse a stream plume puffing from geologic vents, Highway 203 leaves 395 for the year-round resort area of Mammoth Lakes.

Mammoth Lakes

Famous for its world-class winter ski resort, the town of Mammoth Lakes — as its name suggests — also owns a long-standing reputation among sport fishermen and campers for its access to pristine mountain lakes, trout streams, and high country wilderness. Since the 1930s tourists and sportsmen have been drawn to the Mammoth Lakes area by its spectacular outdoor recreational opportunities. While winter weekend visitors often fill the town to capacity, nearly as many people enjoy the Mammoth Lakes area during the summer months.

Today in Mammoth tennis, motocross racing, hot air ballooning, mountain-biking, and triathlons join a healthy list of adventuresome summer activities including horseback riding, backpacking, fly-fishing, boating, swimming and mountain climbing. Summer festivals and concerts bring many talented performing artists to the region. Hiking and photography are fantastic year round, especially spring and fall. Nordic skiiers have discovered the beauty Mammoth Lakes' winter wonderland offers away from the downhill slopes, and helicopter skiing has expanded the horizons of adventure for alpine enthusiasts.

Mammoth Mountain ski area operator Dave McCoy installed his first permanent rope tow on Mammoth Mountain immediately after

World War II, and obtained the Forest Service permit for his full-scale operation at Mammoth Mountain ski area in 1953. Chair One opened on Thanksgiving Day, 1955. McCoy's coaching success helped put Mammoth on the map as a great ski area — his skiiers won races across the country and in Europe. At present the ski area at Mammoth Mountain covers over 3,200 ski-able acres: it includes 30 lifts, three day lodges, four ski shops, snack bars, cafeterias, video services, a ski school, a race department, lockers, hotel and condominium accommodations, two restaurants, a game room, and day care for children. Dave McCoy's future dreams include the development of neighboring June Mountain Ski Resort and a possible expansion project joining it with Mammoth Mountain to form one of the largest ski areas in the world.

Dayhikers, serious backpackers, and mountaineers have discovered numerous trailheads in the Mammoth area suitable for short excursions or extended treks into the Sierra high country. Whether they seek an afternoon adventure in the mountains, a trans-Sierra route to Yosemite National Park, or wish to explore remote reaches of the John Muir and Pacific Crest Trails, backcountry enthusiasts find Mammoth an excellent place for setting out, refueling, or for their journey's ending. Experienced horse packers guide day rides and fully-equipped expeditions into alpine wilderness. Mammoth area backcountry trails continue to attract ski-mountaineers and ice-climbers during winter months.

The town of Mammoth Lakes provides a complete range of accommodations and entertainment. It is an excellent base for day trips to scenic and historic sites of the Eastern Sierra. Crystal Crag's rocky pinnacle towers above the glittering, crystalline lakes of Mammoth Lakes Basin only a few miles up the Lake Mary road from town. Mammoth City, a long-

Bear Creek Spire and the Pacific Crest reflected in Little Lakes Valley.
ED COOPER

Left: Evening glow on
Ediza Lake in the
Minarets Wilderness.
DENNIS FLAHERTY

Right: Aspens line
Laurel Creek below the
Mammoth Crest.
LARRY ULRICH

deserted mining town, once housed over a thousand miners and sported 22 saloons. The stream-laced meadows of Old Mammoth and the Sherwin Creek area offer even more alternatives for hiking and fishing. Leaving Highway 203 between Mammoth Lakes and the ski area, a six-mile drive called the Mammoth Scenic Loop winds through lodgepole and Jeffrey pine forests and passes very near the lake-bejeweled Inyo Craters to connect with Highway 395 below the Crestview rest area.

Minaret Summit

A sunset view from the vista point at Minaret Summit presents a colorful conculsion to a Sierra afternoon. In the clearing of a storm, brilliant bands of light splinter and scorch scattering evening clouds with rich oranges, lavenders, and reds as a burning sun drops behind volcanically-formed pinnacles of the Minaret Range in the Ansel Adams Wilderness. On a quiet day, the cobalt blue dome of the sky shifts silently through a dozen lighter and deeper velvet shades, then gives way slowly to the darkling night and the emerging stars as the rugged peaks grow rosy with alpenglow.

The road from Mammoth Lakes to the 9,265-foot high Minaret Summit passes the exposed crevasse of an earthquake fault and continues past the Mammoth Mountain ski area. Evening hikers on the marked nature trail at the Summit enjoy views of the dramatically-silhouetted skyline of the Minarets. A picnic area and parking are provided for visitors riding the shuttle bus into the canyon of the San Joaquin River.

Devils Postpile National Monument

A shuttle bus system to Red's Meadow and Devils Postpile National Monument operates during peak summer months to lessen the impacts of motor vehicles on the fragile ecosys-

tem of the canyon. Reducing traffic also allows visitors to listen more closely to the music of birdsong, laughing waters, and whispering pines as they stroll along the shady trails. Convenient and economic, the shuttle bus trip is also an excellent opportunity to relax and enjoy thick forests, wildflowers, and wildlife on the way to colorful meadows, lakes, and falls along the San Joaquin River.

Several campgrounds and picnic areas lie along the river. Backcountry trails lead to alpine lakes in the Ansel Adams Wilderness and the Minaret Range. Cabins and supplies are available at Reds Meadows Resort. Pack trips leave stations at Agnew and Red's Meadows for the high country; shorter day-rides explore the Postpile area. A short but steep trail from the Red's Meadows shuttle stop, last on the line, one and a half miles to Rainbow Falls where the full force of the San Joaquin River tumbles 101 feet over an impressive lava ledge and stirs prisming mists into the afternoon sunlight.

The strangely geometric columns of Devils Postpile formed when great flows of lava, some a thousand feet in depth, poured over the area and then cracked while cooling. The distinct patterns of the fractures resulted from the evenness of stresses caused by uniformities of the material and temperatures in the shrinking

Above: Skiiers at Mammoth Mountain enjoy winter views of the Minarets.
LARRY ULRICH

Left: Geothermal forces beneath the sleeping mountains boil up at Hot Creek.
FRANK S. BALTHIS

Top: Geometric columns of volcanic basalt at Devils Postpile.
LARRY ULRICH

Center, right: The San Joaquin River cascades over a hundred feet at Rainbow Falls.
ED COOPER

Bottom: Inyo Craters, result of recent volcanic activity.
CARA MOORE

lava. Later, glaciers tore away whole sections of the flows, and exposed and polished the sheer columns of basalt. The evidence of such massive volcanic activity serves to remind visitors that the huge mass of Mammoth Mountain itself conceals a dormant, though not necessarily dead, volcano.

June Lake Loop

North of Mammoth Lakes, shortly after Highway 395 begins its drop from the 8,041-foot summit of Deadman Pass into the Mono Basin, Highway 158 makes a 16-mile loop side trip

through June Lake Village and around June, Gull, Silver and Grant Lakes. A magnificent view of Carson Peak, and the westward panorama as well, may cause first-time visitors to stop at the vista point at "Oh! Ridge," on the summit of the incline from June Lake Junction. The beauty of June Lake reveals subtle and different dimensions with each of the seasons.

June Lake offers year-round resort facilities, accommodations and restaurants. Forest Service campgrounds, trailer parks, and rental cabins are scattered along the June Lake Loop. The ski area at June Mountain covers 340 skiable acres, includes eight lifts and a base lodge, and provides a pleasant, smaller-scaled alternative to its larger neighbor at Mammoth Mountain. Other winter sports include snowboarding as well as tobogganing, sledding, and cross-country skiing. Summer activities include bicycling around the loop, all types of fishing, horseback riding and hiking. Scenic backcountry trails leaving from June Lake Loop beckon hikers and climbers even further into the spectacular heart of the Sierra.

Top: Fishing at serene Silver Lake, on the June Lake Loop.
JEFF NICHOLAS

Left: Boaters skim the mirroring surface of June Lake.
CARA MOORE

a deva world of sorts — it's high
    it is a view that few men see, a point
bare sunlight
on the spaces
empty sky
    moulding to fit the shape of what ice left
of fire-thrust, or of tilted, twisted, faulted
    cast-out from this lava belly globe.

—Gary Snyder

A Mountaineer's View of the High Sierra

Top: High above tree line, a land of granite and ice at Arc Pass, John Muir Wilderness.
Gary Ladd

Inset: Climber surveys Humphrey's Basin.
Ken Birchim

Center: Backpackers rest at Muir Hut, along the Pacific Crest Trail.
Pat O'Hara

Right: Legendary climber Norman Clyde, 1885 -1972, pioneered numerous first ascents in the Sierra.
Dick Beach Collection

Opposite: Winter snow
frosting tufa towers of
Mono Lake.
DENNIS FLAHERTY

Above: A window into
the past at the ghost town
of Bodie.
CARA MOORE

CHAPTER FOUR:

The Land of Mono

Between Deadman Pass and Conway Summit Highway 395 traverses the geologically and biologically diverse landscapes of the Mono Basin. This dramatic land of Mono — a land of volcanic craters and cinder cones, a land of an ancient inland sea and strange tufa towers, of cloud-raking peaks and desert vastnesses — has long elicited varied, but always strong, responses from visitors.

In *Roughing It*, published in 1872, Mark Twain emphasized the starkness of the terrain and described the Mono Lake region as "a lifeless, treeless, hideous desert." To Twain, Mono Lake itself was a "solemn, silent, sailless sea" and the "loneliest tenant of the loneliest spot on earth." Evidently missing its beauty, he found it "little graced with the picturesque." On the other hand, Israel Russel, while exploring the Mono Basin for the United States Geological Survey in 1883, discovered much beauty apparently unappreciated by Twain. According to Russel, who later helped to create the National Geographic Society, "few journeys of equal length could present greater diversity in all the elements of scenery than a single summer day's ride from the parched and desert plains bordering Lake Mono on the north, to the

crest of the mountain mass that fills the horizon to the west and southwest of the lake."

Israel Russel described a land of radically contrasting formations and habitats. At one end of the basin he found magnificent mountains "clothed in favored places with forests of pine" reaching far above the timber line and bearing "a varied and beautiful Alpine flora." Here, Russel heard the constant "rush of creeks and rills" from "the canyons that descend from the snow fields and miniature glaciers about the summits." To the east Russel found a stimulating contrast in the parched aridity of the Great Basin. The land of Mono, Russel wrote, contains the "fragments of two distinct geographic provinces. One has the desolation of the Sahara, the other the rugged grandeur of the Pyrenees."

John Muir, so impressed with the scenic value of this region, sought to have Mono Lake included within Yosemite National Park. In 1984 Congress included Mono Lake and most of the nearby Mono Craters in the 116,000 acre Mono Basin National Forest and Scenic Area, the first such designated Scenic Area in the National Forest System.

Mono Lake

Ringed by eeried tufa towers, volcanic craters, mountain peaks, and high desert silences, the saline waters of Mono Lake lay at the heart of this remarkable land. A remnant of the Ice Age, this million-year-old body of water is one of the oldest lakes in North America. Mono Lake has no outlet; over the thousands of years of its existence, salts and minerals washed into the lake have become concentrated as waters have evaporated. Today the lake is much saltier than the ocean and very alkaline. Several volcanic cinder cones in Mono Lake have erupted within the last several thousand years, and hot springs in and around the lake indicate continued volcanic activity in the area. Two intriguing volcanically-formed islands, Paoha and Negit, add to the mystery of the lake. The larger island, Paoha, contains several hot springs and fumeroles — orifices venting heated vapors from deep within the earth.

Though Mono Lake has been called a "dead sea," it actually abounds with life. No fish live in the lake, but the populations of brine shrimp and brine flies adapted to the exceptionally high concentration of salts provide a plentiful food supply for more than seventy species of migratory and nesting birds — including eared grebes, phalaropes, California gulls and snowy plovers — that visit the lake each year. Mono Lake is a critical breeding habitat for the snowy plover, and approximately 90% of the state's population of California gulls hatch here. While the largest numbers of birds can be seen in the summer and fall, the Mono Basin is a part of the larger Owens Valley wintering region. Look for

Opposite, top: Mono Lake twilight silhouette of Pahoa Island.
DENNIS FLAHERTY

Opposite: Western Gull rookery, Mono Lake Tufa State Reserve.
CHUCK PLACE

Opposity, inset: Western Gull chicks.
CHUCK PLACE

Right, top: A view of Mono Lake from atop Mt. Dana, on the Pacific Crest in Yosemite National Park.
JACQUELINE STEURER

Right, below: Glowing rabbit brush and limestone tufa formations along Mono Lake's south shore.
· LARRY ULRICH

red-tailed hawks, rough-legged hawks, golden eagles, Canada geese and other wintering waterfowl.

The density of Mono Lake's salty water gives swimmers a delightful buoyancy, but the salt may also irritate eyes or cuts. Boaters unfamiliar with the lake should stay close to shore and not to attempt a crossing after midmorning or when even a light breeze is blowing. Sudden Sierra winds can easily blow the smooth surface of the lake into an unexpected ferocity rivalling a storm at sea.

The receding waters of Mono Lake leave a shoreline castled and pinnacled with weird towers of tubular lithoid tufa. Tufa towers — which might be regarded as fossilized springs — form as columns of precipitated limestone when calcium-bearing freshwater springs well up into alkaline lake water rich in carbonates. Tufa formation ceases when dropping water levels expose the towers. In 1982 the Mono Lake Tufa State Reserve was established. It protects the spectacular tufa formations exposed by dropping lake water levels since 1941, when Mono Lake's tributary streams were diverted to supply fresh water to the City of Los Angeles.

Tioga Pass — Yosemite

The mountain community of Lee Vining, perched above the shores of Mono Lake, rests near the bottom of the road to Tioga Pass, Route 120, into Yosemite National Park. Modern travelers on the Tioga Road trace a route once traversed by Miwok and Mono Indians trading acorns and obsidian. Early white explorers knew the route as the Mono Trail. In 1883 a mining road finally crossed the mountains — but its hardships were quickly abandoned. In 1915, through the efforts of national parks chief Stephen Mather, the Tioga Road opened to the public. However, this winding highway over the highest automobile pass in California remained unpaved until 1961 and is still closed by winter snows. Pull outs, campgrounds, and trailheads along the Tioga Road give motorists spectacular opportunities to experience a great cross-section of Sierra backcountry.

The Tioga Road approach into Yosemite's Tuolomne Meadows from Mono Basin climbs the Lee Vining Creek drainage past gem-like Ellery and Tioga Lakes. The eastern entrance of Yosemite National Park sits at the 9,945-foot summit of Tioga Pass among the alpine heights of the Sierra. Westbound travelers dropping from the summit into Tuolomne Meadows enjoy sweeping views of glaciated granite peaks and domes, high mountain valleys, forests and meadows. Here the many headwaters of the Tuolomne River gather and begin their descent into the deep inner-mountain gorge known as the Grand Canyon of the Tuolomne. At an elevation of 8,600 feet, Tuolomne Meadows, largest sub-alpine meadow in the Sierra, is a favorite departure and destination point among dayhikers, backpackers, and mountaineers.

Conway Summit

At an elevation of 8,138 feet, Conway Summit north of Lee Vining is the highest point reached by Highway 395 between Southern California and Canada. From the Mono Lake Overview near the summit travelers are treated to a panoramic view of Mono Lake and its islands, the Mono Craters, the basins and ranges to the east, the White Mountains, the Glass Mountains, the high boundary peaks of Yosemite, and the southward marching peaks of the Mammoth crest. At the summit, a high road breaks off westward to the Virginia Lakes area.

Descending from Conway Summit toward Bridgeport, the highway parallels the aspen-lined course of Virginia Creek. Near the historic site of Dogtown — founded in 1857 — only a few ruins of what may have been the first mining settlement to spring up in the region are still visible. Here travelers meet the junction of Route 270 which leads thirteen miles eastward to Bodie State Historic Park.

Bodie

Bodie was founded in 1859 when the discovery of the Comstock Lode at Virginia City started a wild rush to the surrounding high desert country for gold and silver. This raucous boom town reached its notorious heyday by 1879 when Bodie boasted over 10,000 citizens, at least 65 saloons, and only two churches. By 1920 the community had shrunk to less than a hundred residents. Although some mining was

Top, left: Cabins at Twin Lakes, against a backdrop of the Sawtooth Ridge.
ED COOPER

resumed during the Great Depression, Bodie had become virtually a ghost town by the later 1940s.

Bodie State Historic Park, established in 1962, preserves about five percent of the town's original structures in a condition of "arrested decay." Antiquated furniture and merchandise still occupy store windows; household utensils, mining equipment, and old boots lie where they were left; mute grave stones speak of past lives. Though the 486-acre park is open year-round, road conditions are best spring through summer after snows have melted. A self-guided walking tour and a Museum/Visitor Center help visitors interpret the cultural and historic resources of the park. Regarded by many enthusiasts as the largest and best preserved ghost town of the American West, Bodie offers particularly rewarding opportunities for photographers and history buffs.

Bridgeport

Nestled among high, stream-fed pastures surrounding the east fork of the Walker River and Bridgeport Lake, the town of Bridgeport is a gateway to recreational adventures in the northern remoteness of the eastern Sierra. Once a trade and supply center for area mining camps, Bridgeport became the Mono County seat in 1864. Its dignified courthouse, built in 1880, is the oldest still in use in California. The school house, also built in 1880, was converted into the Mono County Museum in 1964. Picturesque ranches provide a pastoral foreground to the rugged Sierra. Nearby rivers, streams, and lakes attract fishermen and boaters. Behind the town the serrated skyline of 12,264-foot Matterhorn Peak and the Sawtooth Ridge invite hikers and campers into the Toiyabe National Forest, the Hoover Wilderness, and the northeastern backcountry of Yosemite National Park.

Top: Photographer's triptych of Bodie. Once a bustling mining center, what remains of this remote ghost town is preserved within Bodie State Historic Park.
JEFF NICHOLAS

Center: The last card game in Bodie . . . residents left all behind for the next boom town gamble.
GARY MOON

Right: Mono County's historic courthouse in Bridgeport.
ED COOPER

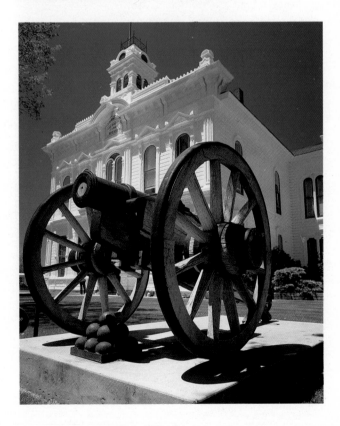

Yosemite National Park Tuolomne Meadows

Above, left: Tuolomne Meadows, guarded by granite and the Cathedral Range.
Ed Cooper

Inset: Lofty Dana Glacier and the icy tarn at its feet.
Jacqueline Steurer-Kemper

Left: Photographing Mt. Gibbs.
Cara Moore

"The Tuolomne Meadow is a beautiful grassy plain of great extent, thickly enameled with flowers, and surrounded with the most magnificent scenery."

— *Joseph Le Conte*
From Rambling in the High Sierra, 1870

Top left: *Ellery Lake along Tioga Pass, approaching Yosemite National Park's East Entrance.*
Cara Moore

Top right: *California Falls, Tuolomne River, in Yosemite National Park.*
Larry Ulrich

Right: *Blooming paintbrush in Tuolomne Meadows, looking toward Lembert Dome.*
Larry Ulrich

CHAPTER FIVE:

Lake of the Sky

*Opposite: Lake Tahoe
beneath winter skies.*
WILLIAM CARR

*Above: Cycling the Flume
Trail, above Lake Tahoe's
eastern shore.*
WILLIAM CARR

From Bridgeport, travelers heading to the Tahoe Basin pass through the shady Jeffrey pine forests of the eastern Sierra's quiet northern reaches. At Devils Gate (elevation 7,591 feet), Highway 395 meets the route followed by legendary scout Kit Carson and Captain John C. Fremont across the Sierra Nevada in the winter of 1844. North of Devils Gate, the highway travels past campgrounds and inviting fishing spots along the Walker River until it meets Monitor Pass, route 89, near Topaz Lake.

Highway 89 leaves the eastern-most slopes of the Sierra and climbs through quaking aspen forests to an elevation of 8,314 feet at Monitor Pass. High in the scenic and once-booming silver country of Alpine County, Highway 89 winds north along the east fork of the Carson River to the town of Markleeville. A museum in Markleeville features Indian artifacts and remnants from colorful silver-rush days. Several of the county's historic buildings — including a blacksmith shop, one-room school, country store, and old jail — have been reconstructed in Markleeville to afford visitors a backward glance into the lives of Alpine's pioneers. Three miles west of Markleeville road-weary travelers can bathe in naturally heated pools at Grover Hot Springs State Park. Leaving Markleeville, Highway 89 continues north through the "California Alps" to the rim of the Tahoe Basin.

Lake Tahoe

"Oh! the exquisite beauty of this lake — its clear waters, emerald-green, and the deepest ultramarine blue . . . the high granite mountains, with serried peaks, which stand close around its very shore to guard its crystal purity; — this lake, not 'among' but 'on,' the mountains, lifted six thousand feet towards the deep-blue overarching sky, whose image it reflects!"

Geologist and explorer Joseph LeConte, recording passionate first impressions of Lake Tahoe in his *Ramblings Through the High Sierra* in 1870, concluded, "I could dream away my life here with those I love." Dreamers and lovers continue to discover and enjoy the sublime beauty of North America's oldest — and perhaps most scenic — mountain lake. Lake Tahoe, described in the journals of John C. Fremont's 1844 expedition, takes its name from the term for "Big Waters" in the language of the Washoe Indians who ritually visit the shores of Lake Tahoe each summer as they have for generations.

Elevated 6,225 feet into rarified alpine air, Tahoe's purity and great depth reflect the

intensity of the atmosphere's brilliant blues with such clarity that Lake Tahoe is known to many as "the Lake of the Sky." Tahoe's 72 miles of shoreline encircle 191 square miles of water surface; the lake's greatest depth reaches 1,645 below. Lake Tahoe formed about 25 million years ago when a dropping fault block between two parallel uplifted fault blocks — the Sierra Nevada to the west, and the Carson Range to the east — created a basin plugged later at its north end by lava flows. Forty percent of the basin's yearly rain falls directly upon the lake's spreading surface; some 63 streams also feed the lake. Continued purity and the crystal clarity of Lake Tahoe's water depend upon careful protection of the basin's air quality and delicate drainage system.

Hiking Around Lake Tahoe

Known for its high concentration of alpine ski resorts, the Tahoe Basin's many trails also draw hikers, campers, and cross-country skiers. The Tahoe Rim Trail is designed to circumnavigate Lake Tahoe with a 150-mile-long ridge top trail. Begun in 1984 with donated funding and volunteer labor, the route links many of the major peaks surrounding the basin and connects segments of pre-existing trail including about fifty miles of the Pacific Crest Trail. The trails, intended for both hiking and equestrian use, may also

be enjoyed by winter cross-country skiers. This impressive, privately organized project involves several administrative agencies and includes stretches of wheelchair-accessible trail, seven trailheads with parking, display maps, educational materials, and rest rooms.

Several other trails await dayhikers in the Tahoe Basin. A well-maintained trail makes a two and one-half mile round-trip from a parking area on Highway 89 at Emerald Bay to the picnic site at Vikingsholm. The Rubicon Trail follows five miles of undeveloped shoreline along Lake Tahoe and Emerald Bay from D.L. Bliss State Park to Vikingsholm. A one-mile hike from the Eagle Picnic Area goes past the cataract of Eagle Falls to Eagle Lake. Glen Alpine Falls at Fallen Leaf Lake is a popular point of entry for backpackers exploring the High Sierra countryof the Desolation Wilderness west of Lake Tahoe.

South Lake Tahoe

South Lake Tahoe has the largest population and concentration of services and entertainment in the Tahoe Basin. Originally

Left: Breaking fresh powder near Emerald Bay. LARRY PROSOR

Right: Celebrating Independence Day at Tahoe City. WILLIAM CARR

Top: Gem-like Emerald Bay, tiny Fannette Island, and the Carson Range behind Lake Tahoe.
PAT O'HARA

Inset: Vikingsholm, a Scandinavian-inspired grand estate, is part of Emerald Bay State Park.
WILLIAM CARR

developed around Lake Tahoe's boating and watersports industry, South Lake Tahoe also attracts winter skiers and offers year-round gambling at casinos just across the California-Nevada state line. The aerial tramway at nearby Heavenly Ski Resort offers panoramic views of Lake Tahoe and the surrounding basin.

A few miles west of South Lake Tahoe on Highway 89 lies Fallen Leaf Lake. According to legend, the lake was formed when an Indian warrior fleeing the Evil Spirit dropped a magic leaf to cover his path. By 1906, the lake had already become a popular resort; many educators and naturalists visited Fallen Leaf Lodge during the teens and twenties.

At the Tallac Historic Site nineteenth-century grand estates, a museum, a Washoe Indian exhibit, and remnants of an historic lakeside resort can be toured during summer months. A stream profile chamber at the Forest Service Visitors Center enables viewers to observe the aquatic life of Taylor Creek. During the annual spawning Kokanee salmon run, usually in October, visitors may watch the bright red salmon digging and defending their nests.

Emerald Bay

The tree-lined shore of picturesque Emerald Bay is protected by D.L. Bliss and Emerald Bay State Parks. Emerald Bay's

sheltered harbor makes a popular destination for boaters and fishermen. Emerald Bay State Park features a boat camping area and other campgrounds, swimming and picnic areas, hiking trails — and one of Lake Tahoe's exceptional grand estates.

Vikingsholm was built as a summer home by Mrs. Lora Knight in 1929. The rugged mountain scenery surrounding the bright emerald waters of the bay reminded Mrs. Knight of Scandinavian fjords and inspired her to design this authentic 38-room reproduction of a Viking castle. Mrs. Knight traveled to Scandinavia to research ideas for construction of her house, and brought skilled old world craftsmen to complete the interior and furnishings. She instructed her architect to preserve the natural environment of Emerald Bay; few majestic trees were cut, and local stone was used in the construction. Mrs. Knight also built a small tea house on Fannette Island — Lake Tahoe's only island — for afternoon boating excursions. Consid-

ered the best example of Scandinavian architecture in the Western Hemisphere, Vikingsholm and its exquisite mountain setting make an intriguing subject for photographers and a choice site for picnicking.

Photographers and sightseers also appreciate nearby Inspiration Point Vista for views of the whole bay. Dayhikers enjoy the short — but steep — trail from Vikingsholm to view Eagle Falls.

Sugar Pine Point

Sugar Pine Point State Park preserves a beautifully forested promontory on the western side of Lake Tahoe. Its attractions include a stretch of lake frontage, the primeval forest of the natural area north of General Creek, a hand-hewn pioneer cabin, and a fine example of the 'opulent' tradition in Tahoe summer homes. Old-growth forests following the drainage to the lakeside include Jeffrey, lodgepole, and sugar pines, plus aspen, cottonwood, mountain alder, and some large Sierra junipers — the largest John Muir said he had seen — near the lake shore.

A sandy beach and pier attract swimmers and fishermen. Phipp's Cabin, built in 1870, was part of the historic homestead of an early Tahoe Basin pioneer, General William Phipps of Kentucky. Elegant Erhman mansion, designed and built in 1901-1903 to be "the finest High Sierra summer home in California," was equipped with the most modern utilities of its day, including electric lights. Today the grand house serves as a visitor center and museum interpreting the history of the Lake Tahoe region.

Truckee

Highway 89 leaves the lake shore at Tahoe City and follows the Truckee River past the Alpine Meadows and Squaw Valley ski areas to meet Interstate 80 near the historic Donner Lake area and the colorful mountain town of Truckee. The Truckee River, the only outlet for Lake Tahoe's waters, flows eastward from Truckee through Reno, Nevada and into Pyramid Lake — never to reach the sea. Donner Memorial State Park offers camping, picnicking, boating, fishing, and water-skiing on Donner Lake. Exhibits at the park's Emigrant Trail Museum interpret natural history of the Sierra, recount the tragic tale of the Donner Party's attempt to cross the mountains here during the savage winter of 1846-47, and tell the dramatic story of how the Central Pacific Railroad was finally built over the forbidding pass.

By 1868 the iron tracks had reached Truckee, a growing, bustling, bawdy town. Today Truckee retains much of its old west flavor; a nostalgic stroll down the sidewalk of Commercial Row takes you back to the late 1800s. Truckee is still a major depot town. About 30 trains come through on the Southern Pacific main line each day; train buffs visit Truckee just to watch them come and go. Several ski areas along Interstate 80 and fine cross-country conditions make Truckee a popular winter resort. The Western America

Left: Boating the extraordinarily clear waters of Lake Tahoe.
WILLIAM CARR

Right: Expert fly fisherman on Spooner Lake, Lake Tahoe's Nevada side.
LARRY PROSOR

Winter contemplation at Sand Harbor, from Lake Tahoe State Park, Nevada.
LARRY ULRICH

Ski Sport Museum at Boreal Ridge features exhibits of skiing history and achievements from 1860 to present.

The North Shore

North Lake Tahoe is a complete year-round resort area with almost limitless recreational opportunities from winter skiing to summer golf and tennis. Enthusiasts join in every imaginable watersport in addition to horseback riding, hiking, camping and more. From rustic cabins to deluxe hotels, North Lake Tahoe provides a diverse selection of lodging and accommodations.

Just over the California/Nevada state line, upscale Incline Village, Nevada was once the site of an incline railroad used in the lumber industry during the 1880s. While in Incline Village, "Bonanza" fans will want to visit the Ponderosa Ranch, permanent home of the Cartwrights, where an entire western town is recreated on the set of this television favorite.

The Nevada Side

Beautiful, white, sandy beaches and translucent blue waters at Lake Tahoe Nevada State Park's Sand Harbor afford idyllic conditions for swimmers and boaters. On warm summer evenings you may catch memorable musical or dramatic perform-ances at Sand Harbor's natural amphitheater. Spooner Lake, also part of the Lake Tahoe Nevada State Park, features catch-and-release trout fishing. Several backcountry trails originate from Spooner Lake including a five mile hike with open views of the Sierra across Lake Tahoe along an old road to Marlette Lake. South of the Highway 50 junction is Cave Rock, an historic Indian site and the reputed home of Tahoe Tessie, Lake Tahoe's equivalent to the Loch Ness monster. A few miles further south, Zephyr Cove is home to a sight-seeing paddleship, a modern reminder of the steamboats that moved timber across the lake in the nineteenth century.

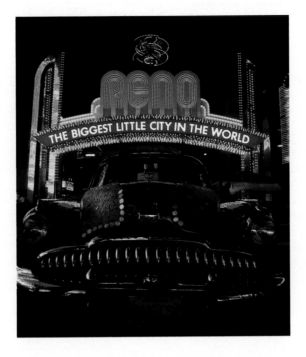

CHAPTER SIX:
Nevada's Silver Country

Opposite: Hot air balloon races at Reno.
WILLIAM CARR

Above: Neon arch welcomes visitors to downtown Reno.
WILLIAM CARR

For many ages only Washoe and Paiute Indians traveled this sage-covered country at the feet of lofty mountains, hunting and gathering in small clans and tribes. In the mid 1840s exhausted emigrants, like the ill-fated Donner Party, first encountered the Eastern Sierra's daunting wall after arduous struggles across the deserts and ranges of the Great Basin. With the history-making discovery of gold at Sutter's Mill in 1848, the arid, high desert lands of Nevada along the mountains' eastern escarpment became a last stop for countless eager miners preparing to cross the final barrier to California's gold fields. With the discovery of gold — and even greater amounts of silver — at the legendary Comstock Lode in Virginia City in 1859, the tide turned. Thousands of prospectors coming across the continent from the east met thousands more crossing the Sierra from the west to Nevada. The Central Pacific Railroad broke through a rugged pass from San Francisco, the forests of Lake Tahoe were logged for timber, mines, fortunes and boomtowns grew, and the once desolate land at the base of the snowy peaks became known to the world as "Silver Country."

Reno

With its reputation as "the Biggest Little City in the World" it is small surprise that Reno's character is a collection of superlatives. World-class hotels feature nightlife, gaming, and big name entertainment. The William H. Harrah National Automobile Museum assembles some of the world's rarest and most expensive cars — including the 1949 Mercury driven by James Dean in "Rebel Without A Cause." Not to be outdone, the Harolds Club gun and weapons collection contains hundreds of antique firearms.

Originally developed as a trading post on wagon train trails, Reno became an important rail head for mines in nearby Virginia City. Guests in this friendly city will find much to do and see. The Nevada Historical Museum displays artifacts from Nevada's frontier past; a special exhibition displays hand-woven baskets of Washoe Indian artists. Fleischmann Planetarium, located on the University of Nevada-Reno campus, presents hemispheric movies and educational programs on astronomy and the natural world. Great Basin Adventure theme park introduces children to Nevada's natural history and the human adventure of old mining days. Wingfield Park, one of several city parks, straddles the Truckee River as it winds through downtown Reno and flows northeast to starkly beautiful Pyramid Lake.

Virginia City

Virginia City is not just the "liveliest ghost town in the west," it is the real thing! Once known as the Queen of the Comstock, this glorious relic of the frontier still reigns in much of her original Victorian splendor from her mountainside throne. "Old Virginny Town" became Virginia City in 1859 with the discovery of the Comstock Lode, one of the richest silver discoveries of the nineteenth century. Profits from the Comstock's ore helped build San Francisco and fund the Civil War. During its boom, boisterous Virginia City bustled with over 30,000 citizens, newspapers, opera houses, Shakespearean theatre, fraternal organizations, saloons, opium dens, and terrific wealth. Samuel Clemens began his career here as Mark Twain while writing for the "Territorial Enterprise."

Visitors today may meander through museums and shops, and among monuments in Virginia City's nine cemeteries where millionaires and paupers lie buried side by side. The Virginia & Truckee steam train, built as a short line railroad to the mines in 1869, still operates excursion service between Virginia City and Gold Hill. The Chollar Mine, founded 1861, gives guided tours of its original shaft. Virginia City's Annual Camel Races commemorate the historic, but ill-fated, experimental effort to introduce these exotic desert beasts as pack animals to the American west.

Carson City

Carson City, Nevada's state capitol since territorial days, invites exploration into the

Top: Fremont Pyramid at Pyramid Lake, final destination of the Truckee River.
ED COOPER

Center: Lincoln Hall, University of Nevada-Reno.
WILLIAM CARR

Left: Weathered downtown establishments along the boardwalk in historic Virginia City.
CARA MOORE

Above: Virginia City, one of the most prosperous boomtowns of the late 1800s, produced vast fortunes in silver ore from her legendary Comstock Lode.
ED COOPER

Right: In Virginia City's heyday, short line steam trains carried ore from the mountain mines. Historic Virignia & Truckee Railroad has been restored for modern-day excursions to "Gold Hill."
CHUCK PLACE

history of the Silver State. From 1870 to 1893 millions of gold and silver coins were struck at the U.S. Mint here — the mint building now houses Nevada's State Museum. Exhibits feature coin presses, the gold-lined silver service from battleship USS Nevada, gaming history, indian basketry, and Nevada's pioneering women. Descend into the museum's re-created silver mine before leaving historic Nevada for the present day. A walking tour of downtown Carson City visits historic mansions built by mining magnates. The silver-domed capitol building is a working government seat as well as a museum; the old senate and assembly chambers are open to visitors.

The Nevada State Railroad Museum houses a collection of Virginia & Truckee Railroad equipment, including restored — and operating — locomotives, passenger and freight cars. The Virginia & Truckee short line served western Nevada and the rich mines of the Comstock from 1869 to 1950. Many of its "rolling national landmarks" had careers in Hollywood films after silver boom days. Visitors journey into railway history on the steam-powered Virginia & Truckee train or motorized car *Washoe Zephyr*.

Southwest of Carson City, picturesque Genoa still boasts old-west store fronts and Nevada's oldest saloon. Rejoin Highway 395 to reach Minden and Gardnerville, nestled in the broad green pasture lands ringed with mountains. Enjoy the flavor of Carson Valley's sheep herding legacy at one of the area's Basque restaurants. Southbound travelers are treated to stunning silhouettes of the Sierra. The sparkling blue waters of Topaz Lake at the Nevada/California border invite swimmers, boaters, skiers and fishermen.

Above, left: Nevada's silver-domed state capitol building, Carson City.
CARA MOORE

Center, top: The artistry of Washoe Indian basketmakers, on display at the Nevada State Museum.
CHUCK PLACE

Center: Descend into a recreated silver mine at the Nevada State Museum.
CHUCK PLACE

Above: 13,140-foot Boundary Peak in the White Mountains, Nevada's highest mountain summit, lies east of the High Sierras and commands views of the Great Basin country.
ED COOPER

Right: A restored steam locomotive at the Nevada State Railroad Museum is a working reminder of the early railway network that helped mine the riches of the Silver State.
CHUCK PLACE

Great Basin National Park

The Great Basin — actually a series of many basins and mountain ranges — extends across western Utah and much of Nevada before terminating at its western boundary, the Sierra Nevada. At this challenging country's heart a new national park was created in 1986. Located in eastern Nevada southeast of Ely, Great Basin National Park protects an extensive limestone cavern and 77,092 acres of sensitive wildlife habitat from desert sagebrush to alpine tundra.

Lofty Wheeler Peak, at 13,063 feet, shelters a trio of crystalline alpine lakes and a glacier on its northeast slope — reminders of the glacial ages that carved these mountains. Below the glacier's rocky terrace, ancient bristlecone pines cling tenaciously to the mountainside's glacial moraine. Local rancher and miner Absalom Lehman discovered a large cave system on the mountain's lower slopes in 1885, and first explored its underground passages. Centuries of slow chemical reaction between acidic water and limestone formed the cave chambers and delicate, colorful stalactites and stalagmites. Join ranger-led tours of Lehman Caves to experience this mysterious subterranean world.

Above left: The glacial face of Wheeler Peak shelters a forest of hardy bristlecone pines.
LARRY ULRICH

Above, Right: Hiking high meadows below Wheeler Peak.
GARY LADD

Left: Exploring Lehman Caves' limestone formations.
LARRY PROSOR